Women
Who
Ruled the
Seas

Women Who Ruled the Seas

Chris Bradford

Illustrated by
Monique Steele

Collins

Contents

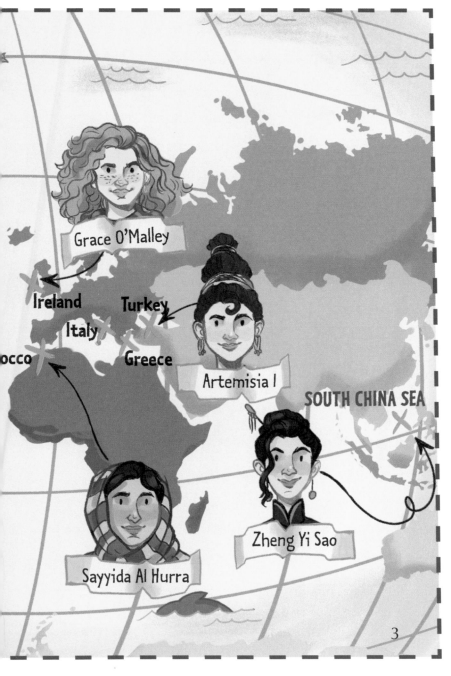

Grace O'Malley

Ireland

Turkey

Italy

occo

Greece

Artemisia I

SOUTH CHINA SEA

Zheng Yi Sao

Sayyida Al Hurra

3

Chapter 1 Ahoy there!

Ahoy there, me hearties! My name is Pearl. I'm not called that because I'm precious, but because I'm hard, and you can find me at sea. My great-great grandmother was the fearsome pirate Saltwater Sally. You haven't heard of her? Well, I'm not surprised. You see, most people think that pirates were *all* men. And that's simply not true! There have been lots of women pirates all through history and around the world. You just might not have heard of them. Now, if you'll be willing to join my crew, I'll take you on a voyage to meet these forgotten female pirates. So jump on board and let's cast off!

What is a pirate exactly?

Good question, ye **landlubber**! A pirate is someone who attacks and robs ships.

By the way, if you sometimes don't understand what I'm saying, there's a Pirate Lingo page at the back of this book you're holding.

I know, that's not very nice. In fact, it's criminal! And I'm not here to defend their actions, but I do want to balance the scales and tell the untold tales of female pirates.

To be honest with you, many of their actions were terrible. I'll explain why each of them became sea **raiders**. This way you can learn more about these women left out of history and you can understand their reasons for becoming pirates.

You see, in books and films, pirates are often shown to be swashbuckling heroes or villains. The truth is that many were ordinary people both men and women who were forced into piracy to survive in harsh times. I admit some were plain nasty, but a few were fighting for a good cause. And every pirate faced prison or even death if they were caught, so becoming one was not an easy decision.

When did pirates first appear?

Piracy goes all the way back to the Bronze Age, which was over 3,200 years ago. Later, there are stories of "Sea People" raiding the ports and ships of Ancient Egypt. Being a pirate was clearly a popular job – many people wanted to do it. In Ancient Greek times, piracy was even seen as an honourable way to make a living!

That opinion didn't last long, of course. The Romans had serious problems with pirate raids – and as a young man, the emperor Julius Caesar was actually captured by pirates! He was held for over a month before a **ransom** was paid for his release. After that, the Romans waged war on the pirates and defeated them in just three months!

Was that the end of piracy?

Definitely not, that was just the beginning!
Pirates continued to **plunder** ships and ports
around the world from China to India, Europe
to the Caribbean. Piracy reached its peak in
the 17th century with the so-called "Golden
Age of Piracy". This was the time of some
of the most famous **buccaneers** in history
– Blackbeard, Captain Kidd, Bartholomew
"Black Bart" Roberts, Calico Jack …

What about famous female pirates?

Ah, now that's the heart of it! There aren't
many mentioned in the history books.
The simple reason is that, in the past, women
weren't allowed to sail, which made it pretty
hard for them to become pirates!

Superstitious sailors believed that having a woman onboard was bad luck. They thought it would make the "water gods" angry, so these water gods would cause storms and sink ships. Others thought women would distract male sailors on long voyages. These are the same people who believed that bananas should not be brought on board either, because the yellow fruit might cause shipwrecks and scare off the fish!

But this didn't stop all women from becoming pirates. To get onboard, some women disguised themselves as men, while others proved themselves in battle. Some female pirates used their power as queens, and some simply ignored the rules. The women I'm going to tell you about may not be widely known now. But in their day, they would have been some of the best-known people ever to have sailed the seven seas.

The Jolly Roger

The most recognised symbol of piracy is
the Jolly Roger – a black flag with a white skull-
and-crossbones. It was raised when a pirate ship
was about to attack. Sometimes this alone was
enough to scare a captain into surrendering.

The Jolly Roger was used regularly during the Golden Age of Piracy. A number of pirate captains flew this flag, including Black Sam Bellamy and Edward England.

But the skull-and-crossbones wasn't the only flag design that pirate ships used. There were different flags that they flew, and the symbols on them meant different things. A plain black flag stood for the death of a crew member, an hourglass showed the quick passage of time, and a wounded heart meant danger.

Are there still pirates today?

You're full of questions, young sea dog! I like your curiosity. Yes, there are. Pirates still operate in many places around the world, particularly in the Indian Ocean. There is now an International Task Force of armed ships protecting these waters.

Timeline of female pirates

Artemisia I of Caria
(520–460 BCE)
Eastern Mediterranean

Sayyida al Hurra
(1485–1561)
Western Mediterranean

Grace O'Malley
(1530–1603)
West Ireland

600 500 400 300 200 100 1000

BCE

Anne Bonny and Mary Read
(1702–1782)
Caribbean Sea

Zheng Yi Sao
(1775–1844)
South China Sea

1200   1300   1400   1500   1600   1700   1800   1900

CE

Chapter 2
Artemisia I of Caria

GREECE

Athens

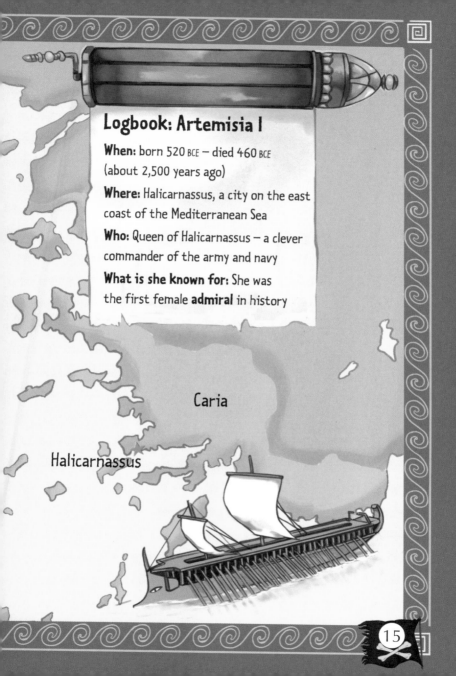

Logbook: Artemisia I

When: born 520 BCE – died 460 BCE
(about 2,500 years ago)

Where: Halicarnassus, a city on the east
coast of the Mediterranean Sea

Who: Queen of Halicarnassus – a clever
commander of the army and navy

What is she known for: She was
the first female **admiral** in history

Caria

Halicarnassus

15

We'll begin our voyage with this queen of the seas — Artemisia I of Caria.

She ruled the city of Halicarnassus in Caria, which is now part of Turkey.

Artemisia was a bold and brave leader. During the war between the Persians and the Greeks, she chose to join the Persian side to try and keep her country safe. She was the only female commander in the Persian navy, and she captained her ships in two great sea battles against the Greeks.

To the Persian King Xerxes and the people of Halicarnassus, Artemisia was a courageous queen. But to her enemy (the Greeks), she was a dangerous pirate.

What was she like?

Artemisia was **cunning**. One of her tactics was to sail with two different flags onboard – Greek and Persian. When approaching a Greek ship, she would raise the Greek flag. They would think that she was a friend – until her ship got close enough. Then Artemisia would make a surprise attack.

This trick helped the Persians win the Battle of Artemisium in 480 BCE. After three days of fighting, the Greeks were forced to retreat.

Friend or foe?

Greek flag raised

Persian flag hidden below deck

I bet the Greeks didn't like that!

No, they were furious – especially when they discovered a woman had outwitted them at sea. So they offered a reward for anyone who could capture her – dead or alive. The reward was 10,000 drachma, which was about three years' wages for a worker. But no one was able to capture Artemisia and the prize remained unclaimed.

Her claim to fame

There was no reason for a queen like Artemisia to go into battle herself – Xerxes certainly didn't! It was highly unusual for either kings or queens to fight. So, it was probably Artemisia's own decision to lead her ships into battle. It showed how determined she was – and as a result, she became the first female admiral ever recorded in history.

Against the queen's advice

Xerxes fought the Greeks and took over much of their land, including Athens, their most important city. But he was keen to finish off the Greeks by fighting them at sea. He called a meeting with his commanders to discuss his plans. Artemisia was the only one to advise against doing this. She urged him to attack on land again, telling him "our enemies are much stronger in the sea than us ... why run the risk of a sea battle?"

Xerxes listened, but he decided to stick with his plan.

So what happened?

Artemisia was right. The Greeks were more skilful sailors. During the Battle of Salamis, they tricked the Persian **fleet** by pretending to retreat, and then launching a surprise attack. The Greek ships moved fast. They quickly caused huge damage to the Persian ships, which couldn't move so quickly.

During the battle, Artemisia's flagship was chased by a Greek boat. The queen was blocked in by Persian ships, and with the enemy right behind her, she decided to try something risky. She rammed a Persian ship and sunk it!

Wasn't the King of Persia angry?

No, in fact he was delighted. You see, he didn't really understand what Artemisia had just done.

Xerxes was watching from a long way away, and he thought that Artemisia had sunk one of the Greek enemy ships. He even praised her for her nerve and daring. Since no one from the rammed ship survived, he never found out that she had actually sunk a Persian ship.

The Greeks were also confused. They could see that Artemisia had rammed a Persian ship, so they thought she must have swapped sides to fight for them, and they left her ship alone.

Artemisia benefitted twice from her risky action. First, she escaped and saved her crew from being killed by the Greeks. Secondly, she got a big reward from King Xerxes – a full suit of Greek armour.

Unfortunately, the battle didn't go the Persians' way. They were defeated and Xerxes eventually gave up his invasion of Greece.

More than just a name

Much of what we know about Artemisia comes from the works of Herodotus, the ancient Greek historian.

" I pass over all the other officers because there is no need for me to mention them, except for Artemisia ... She took over after her husband's death, and although she did not have to join the expedition, her courage impelled her to do so ... Hers was the second most famous squadron in the entire navy ... None of Xerxes' allies gave him better advice than her. "

Herodotus

The remarkable fact here is that Artemisia's name is mentioned while her husband's is not. When so much history has been written about men by men, Artemisia stands as a rare example of a woman who is remembered in history for what she did, rather than who she married and how many children she had.

The pirate code

You may believe pirates were an unruly lot. But in fact, they often had very strict rules. Many captains made their crew members sign the ship's charter — a list of rules they had to obey.

The pirate Bartholomew "Black Bart" Roberts had the following rules aboard his ship, *Royal Fortune*. Would you agree to them?

That last rule is a real kicker for any wannabe female pirates. However, the pirate Zheng Yi Sao had different rules. Women were allowed to stay on board, and the men had to respect them. Anyone who dared to mistreat a woman would be punished severely. Now that's a rule I'd be happy to agree to!

Black Bart's rules for *Royal Fortune*

1 Every crew member to have an equal vote on what we do; also an equal right to fresh food and water.

2 Every pirate to get a fair share of the **loot**. But if any man robs another, they shall be **marooned**.

3 Any crew member that leaves the ship or runs away from battle will be punished by death or marooning.

4 Keep your weapons clean and ready for action at all times.

5 No fighting among the crew on board ship. Any disputes to be settled on shore.

6 Candles to be put out by eight o'clock at night.

7 Musicians are allowed to rest on Sunday. Everyone else must work, every day!

8 And above all, don't allow women on the ship or among the crew. Breaking this rule is punishable by death!

Chapter 3
Sayyida al Hurra

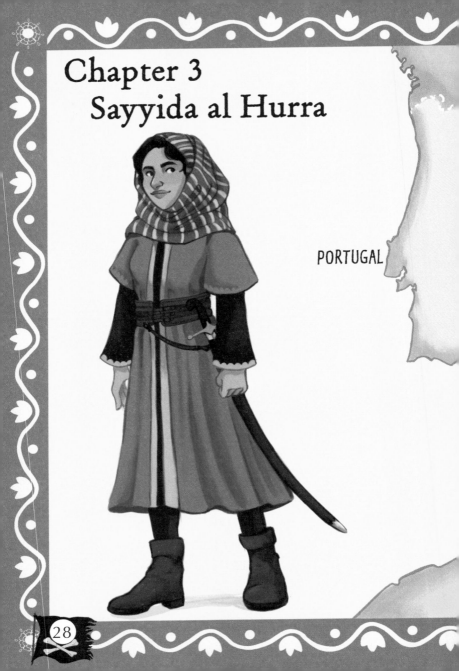

PORTUGAL

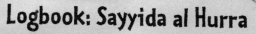

Logbook: Sayyida al Hurra

When: born 1485 – died 1561

Where: Morocco and western Mediterranean Sea

Who: Queen of Tétouan – and defender of her Moroccan city-state

What she is known for: She was a governor and one of the most important female figures in Islamic history

SPAIN
Granada

Tétouan

Fez

MOROCCO

ALGERIA

Next stop on our journey is in Morocco – about 2,000 years after Artemisia sailed the seas. Here we meet Sayyida al Hurra, the avenging pirate queen!

Her birth name was actually Lalla Aicha bint Ali ibn Rashid al-Alami. But history remembers her by her title – *Sayyida al Hurra* – which means in Arabic "a noble lady who is free and independent". It's a term used for female leaders who hold power in their own right. Sayyida more than earned it as the governor and Queen of Tétouan, and she is the last woman in Islamic history to officially hold the title of *al Hurra*.

What was her life like?

A mix of tragedy and good luck. Sayyida al Hurra was born into a noble Muslim family around 1485, in Granada. Granada was a Muslim state in the south of Spain. This Muslim state was attacked by the rulers of Spain, who were Christians, and Sayyida and her family were forced to flee.

Imagine you're seven years old, living a happy, comfortable life with your family and friends. Then suddenly, you have to leave everything behind to go on the run, simply because of your beliefs. This is what happened to the young Sayyida, and it's thought to have lit the fire of revenge in her heart.

Where did she escape to?

Sayyida and her family fled to Morocco, a country in North Africa, where they settled in a city in the mountains. It turned out to be a good life, although Sayyida never forgot the pain of being forced to leave her home.

Her father was an important man, so Sayyida was given a first-class education and she was clearly a bright student. She studied mathematics and politics, and learnt several languages including Spanish and Portuguese. These lessons prepared her well for her future as a ruler.

How did she become Queen of Tétouan?

Around 1501, Sayyida married a man called Abu Hassan al-Mandari. He was the governor of the city of Tétouan on the coast of Morocco. Abu Hassan was also a refugee from Granada, so this is something they had in common. It seems clear that Abu Hassan respected and admired Sayyida, because whenever he went away on a trip, he left her in charge.

Together, they helped rebuild the city into an important seaport complete with a mosque where all Muslims could worship.

By the time her husband passed away in 1515, Sayyida was a respected and successful leader in her own right, worthy of the name *al Hurra*.

I thought you said she was a pirate?

I did – and her status as Queen may be another reason why. As a woman in a time when it was really only men who held positions of power, Sayyida was already accepted as a ruler. You see, the fire of revenge had been slowly growing in her heart. Sayyida had not forgiven the Spanish and Portuguese rulers for forcing her family out of Granada all those years ago. In her desire for revenge, she turned to piracy.

Sayyida joined forces with the fearsome Oruç Reis, better known to the Western world as the pirate Barbarossa. Sayyida and Barbarossa agreed that Barbarossa would

raid enemy settlements in the east of
the Mediterranean, around Italy and Greece.

Meanwhile, Sayyida's pirate fleet would target
the west of the Mediterranean, around Spain
and Portugal. This allowed Sayyida to attack her
old enemies and become the undisputed pirate
queen of the western Mediterranean.

Sayyida soon earned a reputation as fearsome as Barbarossa's. She also became extremely wealthy. Her pirates seized huge amounts of treasure, and she also captured Spanish and Portuguese prisoners and held them to ransom for lots of money.

One Portuguese official at the time called her "a very aggressive and bad-tempered woman". I think he was a little sore at the huge losses his country was suffering. She returned the prisoners once their ransom was paid.

The Sultan of Fez, on the other hand, thought Sayyida was wonderful. He even made a 270-kilometre trek from Fez to Tétouan just to marry her. This was a highly unusual thing for an important ruler to do. It's a clear sign of Sayyida's power and influence.

A woman ahead of her times

During an age in history when the world
was ruled mostly by men, Sayyida al Hurra
is a rare example of a powerful woman.
Her journey from refugee to queen is quite
an achievement. Highly educated, she was
a clever businesswoman, a respected leader
and the commander of a feared fleet of pirates.
Many people today believe that she deserves her
title of al Hurra.

Mythbuster!
Did pirates have eye patches and hooks?

Yes, some did! Life at sea was harsh. Battles and fighting caused many injuries and sailors could lose arms and legs. In fact, Sayyida's partner-in-crime, Barbarossa, had a silver false arm. Some pirates would wear patches to cover missing or damaged eyes. These patches could also help with night vision. A pirate would cover one eye on deck and then lift the patch as they went below deck so they could see better in the darkness.

Chapter 4 Grace O'Malley

Doona Castle

Clare Island
(Granuaile's Castle)

Burrishoole
Castle

Hen's Castle

Logbook: Grace O'Malley

When: born 1530 – died 1603

Where: Ireland

Who: a rebel and defender of the Irish coast

What she is known for: She was a soldier and politician and some saw her as a national hero of Ireland

IRELAND

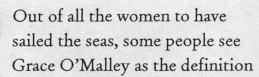

Out of all the women to have sailed the seas, some people see Grace O'Malley as the definition of a pirate: fierce and formidable. In Ireland, she is still remembered in folk songs, stories and even statues.

Grace O'Malley was leader and a rebel. A soldier and a mother. A politician and a pirate. Grace O'Malley (*Gráinne Ní Mháille* in Irish) is seen as a symbol for Ireland. At a time when much of her country fell under English rule, she alone successfully defended her lands.

Why have I not heard of her?

She was almost written out of history. You see, Irish historians in the past wanted Gaelic women to be seen as obedient, loyal and doing as they were told. Grace didn't fit that mould and so they left her out of their writing. Folklore and stories keep Grace's memory alive.

In fact, Grace never fitted any mould. Born around 1530 to a seafaring clan who ruled over the west coast of Ireland, she was eager to prove herself from a young age. When Grace's father wouldn't allow her on a trading expedition, explaining that her long red hair would get caught in the ship's rigging, Grace promptly chopped all her hair off and sneaked onboard the ship anyway.

This act of rebellion earned her the nickname "Grace the Bald".

What did Grace do next?

Her time at sea gave her the skills, strength
and confidence to be a sailor. But she was
still too young to command her own fleet.
In 1546 at 16 years old, she married
Donal O'Flaherty who was the son and
heir to the powerful O'Flaherty clan.
When Donal O'Flaherty was killed by a rival
clan in 1565, Grace inherited his ships and
castle, which she defended fiercely from attack.

On the death of her father in the 1560s,
Grace then took over as leader of the O'Malleys.
She gained command of a fleet of 20 ships and
200 men. She used these to raid English boats
and demanded money from them for sailing
near the Irish coast.

So, she was a real pirate?

Absolutely! In battle, she fought with pistols and a cutlass. One story tells of how she gave birth to her son Tibbot at sea. The next day, enemy pirates attacked their ship. Wrapping her newborn son in a blanket, Grace appeared on deck, gun in hand. She rallied her crew and captured the pirate vessel.

With castles, ships and followers of her own, Grace was seen as a true Irish defender by her people. She was also a successful businesswoman. With her second husband, she made money selling goods to Spain and Portugal. Around this time, the English were trying to take over Ireland, and Grace joined other Irish rebels in fighting against them.

None of this, of course, went down well with the English, and in an effort to stop her, the English commander Sir Richard Bingham ordered the murder of her oldest son. He then took her lands and castle by force and kidnapped her younger son Tibbot.

In order to save Tibbot's life, Grace set out on her most difficult voyage yet. She sailed to London to demand his release from the woman in charge of England – Queen Elizabeth I.

In September 1593, Grace met the Queen at her court in Greenwich Palace. Supposedly, Grace refused to curtsy because she wouldn't recognise Elizabeth as the "Queen of Ireland". She also thought herself to be Queen Elizabeth I's equal.

It may be that Queen Elizabeth I was impressed by this strong-willed woman, since she set Tibbott free and ordered Bingham to return Grace's castle and lands. In exchange, Grace agreed to stop her pirate attacks on English ships and help fight Queen Elizabeth I's enemies at sea.

Was that the end of Grace's pirating days?

Not exactly. Grace rebuilt her fleet and returned to her lawless ways. But she did keep her end of the bargain and fight on behalf of Queen Elizabeth I against her enemies. It's believed that Grace died around 1603, the same year as Queen Elizabeth's death.

Whether you think Grace O'Malley was a bold leader or a cut-throat pirate, she will always be remembered as strong. Like her family's motto, she was "Powerful by land and by sea".

Mythbuster!
Did pirates bury their treasure?

Legend says that Grace O'Malley buried over nine tons of gold treasure and protected it with a curse. A few other pirates supposedly did too, and one of these was Captain Kidd. He claimed that he'd buried vast amounts of plunder, and for centuries, treasure hunters tried to track it down. But it wasn't common practice. Many pirates died young, so they wanted their share of the spoils right away and tended to spend it fast. Also, a lot of the loot was more everyday items, such as spices, timber, cloth and animal skins. Burying such loot would ruin it!

Chapter 5
Anne Bonny and
Mary Read

Republic of
Pirates,
Nassau

THE BAHAMAS

Logbook: Anne Bonny and Mary Read

When: active years 1719–1720

Where: Caribbean Sea

Who: an Irish woman and an English woman

What they were known for:
The two most notorious female buccaneers to have sailed the seas

CUBA

JAMAICA
Negril
Spanish Town

Swashbuckler. Sea Raider. **Marauder**. Buccaneer. **Privateer**. No matter what you call a pirate, one thing is certain: they were feared at sea, and none more so than this pair of female pirates.

Anne Bonny from Ireland and Mary Read from England met by chance and became a fearsome pair. Their pirating career lasted a few short, violent months in the year 1719. Yet they left their mark on pirate history.

They sound dangerous. Tell us more!

What little we know about them comes mainly from a book called *A General History of the Pyrates*. It was written in 1724, and it was the first book about some of the most famous pirates of the time – although not everything in it may be true.

What do we know about Anne Bonny?

Anne is said to have been born around 1697 in Ireland. For family reasons, her birth had to be kept a secret. So, when she was a young girl, her father made her dress as a boy and pretend to be his assistant in his lawyer office. When people found out she was a girl and his secret daughter, Anne and her father were forced to move away and decided to go to America.

Here, Anne began to show her "violent temper" when she attacked a servant girl. She also annoyed her father by marrying a poor sailor named James Bonny. Her father disowned her, so she set off with her new husband to the so-called *Republic of Pirates* in the Bahamas in the Caribbean.

That's a wild start to life. What about Mary Read?

She also had an interesting childhood. Born in England in 1685, Mary spent her youth disguised as a boy too. Her mother was a widow and penniless. She forced Mary to pretend to be her own half-brother (who had passed away) so that they could get inheritance money from his grandmother. The trick worked, and they lived off the inheritance into Mary's teenage years.

As she grew up, Mary adopted the name Mark and took on various jobs as a man, first as a servant, then as a soldier and later as a sailor.

It was when she was aboard a ship heading to the Caribbean islands in 1717 that her ship was attacked by English pirates. Disguised as a British sailor, Mary was forced to join the crew and become a pirate herself — or maybe she chose to be a pirate?

How did Anne and Mary meet?

It was a matter of fortune and fate. On arriving in the Bahamas in 1718, Anne soon met the pirate captain "Calico Jack". She joined his crew disguised as a man, and they sailed round the Caribbean stealing from poorly-armed ships. According to accounts, Anne could fight like the best of Calico Jack's crew, if not better.

Mary, having pirated her way to the Bahamas, joined Calico Jack's crew in 1720. At first, she did not realise Anne was a woman. Nor did Anne know Mary's secret. But they soon confided in each other and the deadly team of Bonny and Read was created.

Didn't the crew know they were women?

Most likely. Given the cramped conditions on ship, it would be hard to hide their identities forever. In fact, historical records of the time say Bonny and Read wore women's clothes day-to-day and only dressed as men when they went into battle.

One witness, Dorothy Thomas, described them wearing "men's jackets, and long trousers, and handkerchiefs tied about their heads, and each of them had a **machete** and pistol in their hands."

loose shirts made from cotton or canvas

bandana for keeping sweat off the face

jewels (likely stolen)

belt/sash for keeping the back strong while hauling rope

loose trousers for mobility while working on the ship

What did pirates wear? Often, they would have to disguise themselves and dress like men to get on board. But other female pirates, like Anne Bonny and Mary Read, became bolder and wore their own clothes. They had their own style – flowing jackets, long trousers and handkerchiefs around their heads!

So, they were fighters?

Skilled fighters. Remember, Anne had a temper
and Mary had been a soldier. They were just as
strong as the other pirates. When Calico Jack's
ship, *William*, was taken by surprise by pirate-
hunters in November 1720, only Anne, Mary
and one male pirate fought back.

The two women were furious with
the cowardly crew. When Calico Jack was put
on trial and sentenced to death, Anne had little
sympathy for her captain.

Were Anne and Mary sentenced to death too?

Yes, they were both tried and found guilty of piracy. But their execution was delayed when they begged for mercy because they were pregnant.

Mary died in prison from a fever in 1721.

But there is no record of Anne's fate. Some say she remained in prison. Others say she moved back to America and had eight more children. Yet others believe she escaped to another Caribbean island, changed her name and lived there the rest of her days.

Whatever the truth may be, Anne and Mary's short, savage pirate career has inspired countless stories throughout the centuries.

Bonny and Read's ship – *William*

When we talk about pirate ships, it's important to note that the ships often didn't belong to the pirates. In most cases they were stolen or hijacked. For example, take the ship that Anne Bonny and Mary Read sailed on. The captain, Calico Jack, stole a sloop called *William* from a port in the Bahamas in 1720. Good choice of ship, though!

Pearls of wisdom
- A sloop is a sailboat with a single mast, one headsail and one mainsail.
- It is fast, very mobile and can be sailed with a small crew.
- This makes a sloop the perfect attack-and-getaway ship for a pirate!

Ship stats

Type: Sloop

Length: 7–10 m

Top speed: up to 12 knots
(22 kilometres per hour)

Number of masts: 1

Number of sails: 2

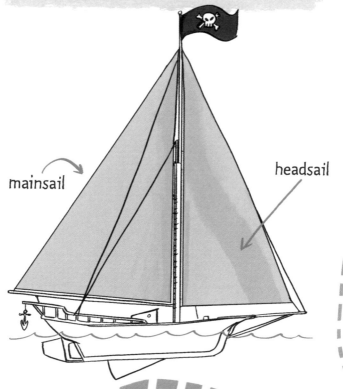

mainsail

headsail

Chapter 6 Zheng Yi Sao

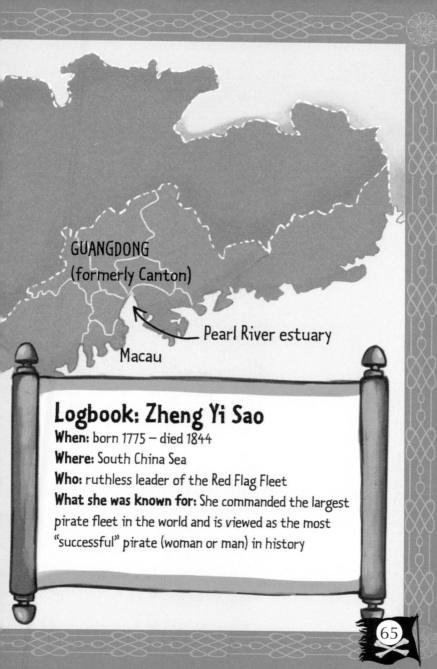

GUANGDONG
(formerly Canton)

Pearl River estuary

Macau

Logbook: Zheng Yi Sao
When: born 1775 – died 1844
Where: South China Sea
Who: ruthless leader of the Red Flag Fleet
What she was known for: She commanded the largest
pirate fleet in the world and is viewed as the most
"successful" pirate (woman or man) in history

All right, shipmates! We're reaching the end of our journey and I've saved Zheng Yi Sao for last. Zheng Yi Sao (as she is most commonly known) was a woman to be feared.

At the height of her power, she commanded a fleet of over 1,000 ships and more than 70,000 pirates. This is the largest pirate fleet the world has ever known.

For almost a decade in the 1800s, Zheng Yi Sao's pirate navy terrorised the South China Sea – and her rule was ruthless and highly organised.

How did she rule?

Zheng Yi Sao ran a tight ship. To manage such a large fleet, she split it into six different-coloured flagged fleets (Red, Black, White, Blue, Yellow and Green) and laid down a set of rules that her pirate crews had to obey, or else!

My Rules ...

1. No going ashore without permission

2. No stealing from the loot

3. Obey all orders

4. Women must be respected at all times!

How did Zheng Yi Sao become so powerful?

That's a good question, because she started life as an outcast. She was born as Shi Yang to a family of "boat people" known as Tankas around 1775 in Guangdong, China. The Tankas lived on their boats at sea and survived by selling fish. In 1801 she married the pirate lord Zheng Yi and her name changed to Zheng Yi Sao, meaning "Wife of Zheng Yi". As his wife, she demanded equal control of his pirate fleet and half the loot.

Together they built a powerful pirate empire.

They plundered their way across Southeast Asia. They attacked Chinese ships carrying silk and spices. They also targeted foreign ships and held the sailors to ransom. Any boat passing through their waters had to pay a fee. And they even raided the coastal towns — no one was safe from them.

Then in 1807 her husband died, and Zheng Yi Sao took over.

Leader of a pirate state

Zheng Yi Sao was a clever leader. She placed relatives in high positions in her fleet so she knew everyone in the fleet would be loyal to her. She put her stepson, Zhang Bao, in charge of the main Red Flag Fleet. She made sure her husband's relatives, who were pirate commanders, backed her. In this way, she held command over the entire "Pirate Confederation" of six fleets.

Zheng Yi Sao became ever more powerful. Her fleet grew bigger than many countries' navies and soon her Pirate Confederation was like a small kingdom. Zheng Yi Sao even controlled the important salt trade in South China by charging ships money to sail through her domain.

71

Couldn't anyone stop her?

Apparently not, although people did try!
In 1808, the Chinese navy lost 62 of
its 135 ships in sea battles with her pirates.
Outnumbered and outgunned, the Chinese
government had to call on the British and
Portuguese navies for help. But even they
couldn't defeat Zheng Yi Sao.

In the end, it was Zheng Yi Sao herself who
ended her reign as the pirate commander of the
South China Sea.

Why would she stop being a pirate?

There were three main factors that encouraged Zheng Yi Sao to stop. Firstly, her two main commanders had begun fighting among themselves and threatening to break apart the Pirate Confederation. Secondly, the new governor of the region, Ba˘i Líng, was trying to stop piracy with promises of rewards and pardons. Thirdly, Zheng Yi Sao realised that the foreign navies would get more involved. So, she surrendered.

Surrendered? But she was at the height of her power!

That's the best time to strike a deal. On 17 April 1810, Zheng Yi Sao sailed her fleet into Canton harbour and delivered her terms of surrender to Ba˘i Líng.

She wanted a full pardon – for herself and all her crews. In exchange for the full pardon, her fleet would give up their ships and weapons. However, they would keep all their stolen loot.

Her pirate crews were to be offered jobs in the Chinese navy, if they wished.

Finally, Zhang Bao would keep a small fleet of 20 boats and be made a naval officer.

She used her influence and power to drive a hard bargain!

1. Full pardon for every pirate

2. Keep all our treasure

3. Give my crew jobs

4. A small fleet of 20 boats

That's my deal –
take it or leave it!

Did Bǎi Líng agree to her demands?

Bǎi Ling probably wasn't keen on rewarding pirates, but he needed to remove Zheng Yi Sao and take back control of the region. He agreed to her terms of surrender – though retirement might be a better description.

What did Zheng Yi Sao do after piracy?

She used her fortune to start a new business in Guangdong. According to all accounts, she lived a quiet life until her death in 1844 at the age of 69.

Zheng Yi Sao's years as a pirate were legendary. No other pirate commanded so many ships or amassed such a large fortune and managed to hold on to it.

At a time when opportunities for women were few, she defied expectations. Zheng Yi Sao was a fierce fighter, a strategic leader and a skilful negotiator.

Zheng Yi Sao's Red Flag Fleet

Zheng Yi Sao commanded the largest pirate fleet in history. With over 1,000 ships, she decided to colour-code her ships. The lead fleet was Red, the others were Black, White, Blue, Yellow and Green.

Pearls of wisdom

- A junk is a Chinese sailing ship with battened sails, a horseshoe-shaped hull and no **keel**.

- It is one of the most efficient ship designs, being fast and highly stable.

- With no keel, junks could enter shallow waters and surprise another ship anchored there.

- The battened sails can be raised and lowered quickly without needing to climb the mast.

- The watertight **bulkheads** divided the hull into sections. If the junk was rammed in battle, the water could only fill the damaged section meaning it was less likely to sink.

Ship stats

Type: junk

Length: up to 70 m

Top speed: up to 14 knots
(26 kilometres per hour)

Mast number: up to 5 (or more!)

Sail number: up to 5

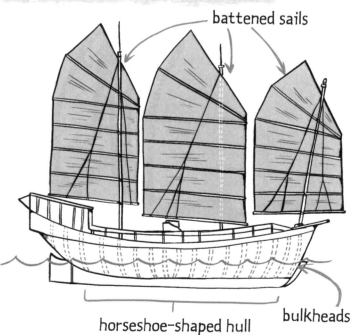

battened sails

horseshoe-shaped hull

bulkheads

Even more female pirates!

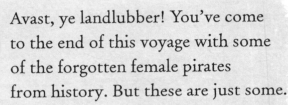

Avast, ye landlubber! You've come to the end of this voyage with some of the forgotten female pirates from history. But these are just some. History is rich with female pirates, if only you look hard enough. Here are a few more …

Sela – A Norwegian sea raider

- She lived about 1,500 years ago.
- Her brother Koller was chief, and she became a pirate to avoid being ruled by him.
- She joined up with another pirate (Horwendil) to take her brother's throne.

Jeanne de Clisson – The French Lioness

- Jeanne lived in the 14th century during the Hundred Years' War between France and England.
- After her husband was executed for treason, she switched sides to fight for the English.
- She had three warships painted black, with red sails.

Rachel Wall – The American

- Rachel was born in America in 1760.
- She is the only American woman ever known to be a pirate.
- She pretended to be in trouble so ships would stop. Then her crew would capture them!

My list could go on! Have you heard of Lady Killigrew, the Elizabethan Cornish privateer? Or Huang Bamei, the modern Chinese pirate who turned down an offer to work for the American CIA? Why don't you carry on the journey and discover more female pirates?

Pirate lingo

So ye want to talk like a pirate? Arrrr, me hearties! Much of the pirate language you may have heard is made up for TV and films – most pirates would have spoken like any normal sailors of their time.

Still, it's fun to speak Piratese. In fact, there's an annual "Talk Like A Pirate Day" on 19th September. So, if you want to learn the lingo, here are a few words and phrases.

Ahoy means "hello" and it's a good greeting to start with.

Arrrr can be used in almost any conversation. Agreeing with someone, expressing pleasure... Feel free to use it any time, **arrrr**!

Avast is shouted to tell someone to stop and listen.

Aye means yes. So never say yes, because other pirates will know you're not a real pirate.

Aye, aye means "I'll get to it". Always say this to your pirate parent when they ask you to do something.

Cap'n is a shortened version of the word "captain". Good for showing respect.

Davy Jones's Locker refers to the bottom of the ocean where shipwrecks end up.

Hang the jib means to frown or pout. Tell that to your matey the next time they're whingeing.

Matey is used to describe a good friend.

Me hearties means my friends, as in "close to my heart".

Old salt is what we call an older, experienced sailor.

Run a rig is to play a joke or trick on someone else.

Shiver me timbers means to destroy a ship. It is a cry of surprise, often when caught off-guard.

Swab the decks is a command to clean the ship.

Weigh anchor is when the captain wants the anchor raised so the ship can set sail.

Arrrr, me hearties, try talkin' with yer matey and see if you can run a rig on 'em!

81

Funny pirates

Here are a few pirate jokes that may tickle your ribs ...

Why don't pirates shower before they walk the plank?

Because they'll just wash up on shore later.

What kind of grades did the pirate get in school?

High Cs!

How do you turn a pirate furious?

Take away the "p".

What's a pirate's favourite letter?

The letter RRRRRR!

What did the ocean say to the pirate?
Nothing, it just waved.

What's a pirate's least favourite vegetable?
Leeks!

Why does it take pirates so long to learn the alphabet?
Because they can spend years at C.

What lies at the bottom of the ocean and looks scared?
A nervous wreck.

Glossary

admiral the top commander of a fleet or navy

buccaneer a pirate operating in the Caribbean, especially in the 17th century

bulkheads dividing walls between compartments inside a ship

cunning to be crafty or sly

fleet a group of ships sailing together under the same command

keel the length of timber along the bottom of a ship, which helps to keep the boat steady

landlubber a person unfamiliar with the sea or sailing

logbook a written record of events during the voyage of a ship

loot items stolen during a war or riot

marooned to leave someone stranded on an island

marauder a person who goes about stealing and attacking people

plunder to steal using force or violence

raiders people who attack enemies in their territory

ransom a sum of money demanded or paid for the release of a captive

privateer a crew member of an armed ship with government permission to capture other ships

swashbuckler a person who goes on daring adventures

About the author

How did you get into writing?

To be honest, I wanted to be a rock star! I was a musician in a band. Then I got the chance to write a book about songwriting, which led onto more music books, and then onto an idea for a story

Chris Bradford

about a young samurai ... and this became a massive bestseller!

Is there anything in this book that relates to your own experiences?

I used to teach sailing, so I know what it's like to be on a ship, to feel the wind in your face and to ride the ocean waves.

What is it like for you to write?

Hard, really hard. Being creative is never easy. Yet the feeling of pride and accomplishment in finishing a book is worth all the effort.

What is a book you remember loving reading when you were young?

I remember my grandad reading *The Adventures of Captain Pugwash* by John Ryan to me at nights. When I was older, I loved *Treasure Island* by Robert Louis Stevenson.

Why this book?

I was inspired to write *Women Who Ruled the Seas* after some research into a pirate queen for my samurai book series. One character I wrote for that was based on the real-life pirate Zheng Yi Sao.

During your research was there anything you found out that really surprised you?

The fact there were so many female pirates. The deeper I dug, the more I found!

About the illustrator

How did you get into illustration?

I have always loved drawing. Growing up, my mum would buy tracing paper for me because I liked to copy the illustrations in all my storybooks. Eventually, I started to draw my own characters.

Monique Steele

What did you like best about illustrating this book?

Imagining what these women would look like was probably the best part for me. I love drawing characters and although these women existed, the only images of them are drawings or paintings.

What was the most diffcult thing about illustrating this book?

Definitely the ships! I did a lot of research to make sure they looked accurate.

Is there anything in this book that relates to your own experiences?

I'm from the Caribbean – Jamaica to be specific, so the golden age of piracy has always been fascinating to me. Getting to draw Anne Bonny and Mary Read was really nice because they operated in the Caribbean Sea and part of their story takes place in Port Royal, Jamaica, so I got to draw a little piece of home.

How do you bring a character to life in an illustration?

The clothes and expressions help to tell a lot about a character. If someone is shy, they won't bring too much attention to them. Small things like that help to make a character feel more real.

Did you have to do any research in order to illustrate this book?

I did a lot of research, particularly on ships and costumes. I watched videos to understand exactly where the bulkhead is on an 18th-century junk ship! The costumes are a similar story. I had to look up how people dressed for each time period. Luckily, I own quite a few books about fashion history and put them to good use!

Book chat

What was the most interesting thing you learnt from reading this book?

If you could ask the author one question, what would it be?

If you could change one thing about this book, what would it be?

If you had to give the book a new title, what would you choose?

Which part of the book did you like best, and why?

Did you know anything about female pirates before reading this book? What do you know now?

Which part of the book surprised you most? Why?

If you could have a conversation with one of the pirates from the book, who would you pick? What would you ask them?

Book challenge: Use pirate lingo to talk about the book.

Collins
BIG CAT

Published by Collins
An imprint of HarperCollins*Publishers*

The News Building
1 London Bridge Street
London SE1 9GF
UK

Macken House
39/40 Mayor Street Upper
Dublin 1
D01 C9W8
Ireland

10 9 8 7 6 5 4 3 2 1

ISBN 978-0-00-862485-9

British Library Cataloguing-in-Publication Data
A catalogue record for this publication is available
from the British Library.

Download the teaching notes and
word cards to accompany this book at:
http://littlewandle.org.uk/signupfluency/

Get the latest Collins Big Cat news at
collins.co.uk/collinsbigcat

Author: Chris Bradford
Illustrator: Monique Steele (Illo Agency)
Publisher: Lizzie Catford
Product manager and
    commissioning editor: Caroline Green
Series editor: Charlotte Raby
Development editor: Catherine Baker
Project manager: Emily Hooton
Content editor: Daniela Mora Chavarría
Copyeditor: Catherine Dakin
Proofreader: Gaynor Spry
Cover designer: Sarah Finan
Typesetter: 2Hoots Publishing Services Ltd
Production controller: Katharine Willard

Collins would like to thank the teachers and
children at the following schools who took part in
the trialling of Big Cat for Little Wandle Fluency:
Burley And Woodhead Church of England Primary
School; Chesterton Primary School; Lady Margaret
Primary School; Little Sutton Primary School;
Parsloes Primary School.